Studying

PSYCHOLOGY

A Manual for Success

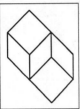

Robert T. Brown
*University of North Carolina
at Wilmington*

Allyn and Bacon
Boston • London • Toronto • Sydney • Tokyo • Singapore

D0066948

Studying Psychology

Studying Psychology
A Manual for Success

Prepared by

Robert T. Brown
University of North Carolina at Wilmington

Allyn and Bacon
Boston • London • Toronto • Sydney • Tokyo • Singapore

Copyright © 1991 by Allyn and Bacon
A Division of Simon & Schuster, Inc.
160 Gould Street
Needham Heights, Massachusetts 02194

All rights reserved. No part of the material protected by this copyright
notice may be reproduced or utilized in any form or by any means,
electronic or mechanical, including photocopying, recording, or by any
information storage and retrieval system, without written permission
from the copyright owner.

ISBN 0-205-13027-5

Printed in the United States of America

10 9 8 7 6 5 4 3 2   95 94 93 92 91

Studying Psychology: A Manual for Success

Table of Contents

Acknowledgements

I thank Dr. Laureen Martin, Dr. William Overman, Ms. Joann Bernat, and especially, Dr. Sue Lamb for their very helpful suggestions concerning the content and writing style of this booklet. I also enjoyed very much working with two people at Allyn and Bacon. Ms. Diana Murphy originally had the idea for this booklet and provided much encouragement and numerous suggestions during its development. Ms. Joyce Tarrio provided excellent (and very tolerant) technical support in getting what I sent to Allyn and Bacon into publishable form.

Studying Psychology

Introductory Remarks

In an old Yiddish joke, an obviously lost tourist in New York asks an old man who is carrying a violin case, "How do you get to Carnegie Hall?" The old man answers, "Practice, my boy, practice...." We take for granted that if you want to play a musical instrument or a sport really well, you are going to have to practice a lot. And those who want to do well willingly spend many hours and days of effort in practice that is not only active, but dull, repetitive, and occasionally painful. Practice mainly the night or two before a concert or game certainly would not do the job. Obviously, no knowledgeable performer or athlete would stay up all night before the big event practicing. Performance would suffer dramatically.

Perhaps you have already seen where this little drama is headed. When learning and remembering course information, students frequently not only try to squeeze studying into an unrealistically small amount of time (consider the common phrase "cramming for an exam") but use inefficient means of studying. Perversely, people who actively practice a sport may also actively avoid effective studying. As an instructor, I am frustrated by this tendency, which all too often leads students to perform far below their own aspirations and abilities. They may, as a result, become frustrated with college and give up on themselves.

Thus, this little booklet, whose purpose is to help you develop skills to learn introductory psychology -- and other topics as well -- more effectively. The analogy of studying with practice will crop up several times. Indeed, one more analogy is appropriate here. Frequently those who want to improve their playing get help from a coach. A good coach should tell you specific ways to improve, pointing out strengths and weaknesses in your current performance. My job is very much like that of a coach, and I will make specific suggestions to help you improve your performance in this course. One obvious difference between me and a coach is that I cannot observe your behavior and comment

1

on it. For this booklet to be of value, you will have to be your own observer and commentator.

Make no mistake, getting good grades on tests and papers involves skills that can be learned and improved just as those involved in sports or music. Indeed, some skills are the same. But let's not kid ourselves: the secret is the same as in the joke -- practice, lots of practice. Reading this booklet will in itself do no more to help you get better grades than would reading a book on golf in itself help your game. Only trying and practicing the suggestions will help. Sorry about that. As my wife, Dr. Sue Lamb, a counseling psychologist, tells some clients, "I don't have any magic pills." Anyone who tries to sell you an easy way to get good grades should have the credibility of someone trying to sell you an easy way to make a million dollars. It should be quite clear who is going to come out ahead. As an example, one advertisement some years ago hawked, "College Level Instant Learning Programs" in basic psychology, chemistry, etc. Sounds great, doesn't it? But it also sold programs on "Instant Piano," "Instant Guitar," and winning roulette at casinos, becoming a witch, and harnessing your psychic powers! So, if you really want to play the learning game, put on your academic sweats and get ready for a little mental perspiration.

Material in this booklet is designed to be specific, applied, and concise. Since whole books are available on each of the topics to be presented, material here will necessarily be condensed. Little theory and only a few references of general interest will be provided. You will see the basis for many of the suggestions to follow in your textbook. We will begin, however, with a few basic principles. Specific applications of many of them will appear in later sections.

Some Basic Principles

These principles summarize basic psychological knowledge of factors that influence how well people perform, particularly those that determine student success in courses. You will find some of the research that underlies these principles in various chapters in your general psychology textbook. What is important here is that psychologists and others have learned a lot about both general factors that are important in success in <u>any</u> endeavor, summarized in 1-5, and specific factors involved in learning and remembering information, summarized in 6-11.

1. *Motivation and goal-setting facilitate active involvement in learning and studying.* Motivation energizes and directs behavior toward a goal. Your text may, at some point, describe evidence that indicated that the single most important factor determining success in a given career is motivation. Without motivation, goal-directed behavior is unlikely to occur, particularly when you have little immediate external pressure to perform. No coach hanging over your head, right?

In practice, motivation to perform well in courses must come from within. Others can try to tell you how important grades are or offer incentives, but the motivation is yours. For that reason, goal setting is crucial.

2. *People who accept responsibility for their behavior perform better -- and generally are happier.* This concept will appear in several places in your text, in descriptions of people high in achievement motivation, of internal vs. external locus of control, and of attribution theory. Basically, people can either accept responsibility for the consequences of their behavior or place that responsibility on some external force, situation, or person. Of particular importance is the attribution of success or failure to one's own effort, discussed in detail in the section on Self Motivation.

3. *What we say to ourselves, particularly about ourselves, is an important factor in our motivation and behavior.* Related to #2, our own messages to ourselves, what some call "self-talk," is an important aspect of attribution. Cognitive-behavioral therapists suggest that it is not what happens to us, but how we interpret what happens to us that determines our emotional reactions and also our behavior. The role of negative and positive self-talk cannot be exaggerated. A constant drumming of negative thoughts sets the occasion for depression, low effort, and poor performance. After all, if you hear someone over and over telling you that you cannot do something, you may well come to believe it. And when you say, "I can't do it," that literally means you are unable to do it. Thoughts like that hardly inspire efforts to succeed.

4. *Both practice and study require effort and time.* Motivation is important because it energizes behavior and fosters task-directed effort. As you would spend many hours in active practice to improve performance in a sport, so you should expect to spend many hours of active study to master material for your courses. Instructors generally expect that you will spend at least two hours out of class for every hour in class. General psychology is typically a three hour course, which means that you should expect to study six hours each week, not just the week before an exam. The major factor in poor student performance is insufficient study. Given individual differences in the human condition, some students will need to spend more time than others studying, just as some need to spend more time practicing to reach a given level of performance in a sport.

5. *Active involvement with material facilitates learning and memory.* Many students are surprised to learn that reading and studying are different activities involving different skills. One studies in order to learn, to understand, and later to be able to remember material and use it to solve problems. Active practice and involvement with that material will improve learning and memory in the same way that practice does in sports or music.

4

6. *Familiarity breeds knowledge.* New information is by definition novel. As such, it may not be understood, let alone learned. Making the material more familiar, even through brief study, is a beginning to knowing it. An analogy with human relationships may fit -- When we meet new people, we have to become familiar with them before we can really know them. Similarly, a musician may scan over a new piece of music before even trying to play it.

7. *Learning and study sessions should be similar to test-taking situations.* In your psychology course, you may learn about transfer of learning. Briefly, the extent to which what you learn in one situation transfers to another depends on a number of factors, among them the similarity of the tasks. The more your studying is similar to your test-taking, the better your knowledge will transfer. As an example, the one behavior common to virtually all tests is answering questions. Answering practice questions during studying helps to ensure that you will later be able to answer questions on the exam.

8. *To organize is to remember.* Familiarity is not enough to ensure either understanding or remembering. An important additional factor is organizing information into meaningful units and concepts. Trying to remember lots of individual facts is difficult and frustrating.

9. *Teaching something to someone else helps you to learn it.* Peer learning is an underused resource. Students may be able to help others understand a topic better and increase their own knowledge. I strongly recommend that students form study groups and meet regularly (not the night before the exam!) to help each other by asking and answering questions and clarifying confusing topics. If confusion cannot be resolved, the problem can then be brought to the instructor, who may be more helpful if he or she sees that you have made a serious attempt to learn it on your own.

10. *Spaced practice is more effective than massed practice.* In sports, music, and academic material, larger numbers of relatively short practice sessions spread out over

time are more effective than a shorter number of longer ones. Frequent study and review are among the most important factors involved in student success. Following a regular schedule for studying, as one would for practicing a sport, facilitates learning.

11. *We can fully attend to only one thing at a time.* Humans are frequently excellent at rapidly shifting attention from one task to another, which may lead to the feeling that we can actually divide our attention. That is apparently not true. If music is playing while you study, to the extent that you actually listen to the music, you will not actually study. Music may be valuable to mask background noises that are even more potent distractors. Thus some people will study more effectively under some conditions with music playing, but not because they can study and listen at the same time. Similarly, those who think that they can fully listen to a lecture while writing or reading a letter are misleading themselves.

Some Simple Suggestions
for Getting Started

Here are a few steps that you can take right at the beginning of the course to help make the rest of the semester easier. They are based on the premise that you have more time now than you will at any later time in the semester. After all, few students have hour exams or term papers in the first week. Extra time spent now is a good investment. Many of you may find them so obvious as not to warrant mention. If so, pass on to the next section. But beware -- they are mentioned because many students have gotten into serious trouble, occasionally resulting in course failure, by having failed to consider them.

1. *Set those long-term and short-term goals mentioned earlier.* One specific goal is to decide what grade you can realistically shoot for in each course and then determine what you need to do actually to get it.

2. *Read your text book for general psychology.* Yes, the whole book, although obviously not word for word. In his delightful and very useful book, Use Both Sides of Your Brain, Buzan (1983) terms this step "the browse." In doing a browse, you skim through the entire book, reading chapter summaries, skimming paragraph headings and first sentences, and looking at tables and figures. Of particular importance, read the author's preface. In this initial browse, you begin the process of becoming familiar with all the material to be covered in the course. You will have an overview of the entire course content at the outset. The browse should not take more than a couple of hours.

3. *Buy the student study guide for the text if it is available.* (No, I don't get a cut of the profits from your bookstore or the publisher!) The guide may be the best investment, other than the text itself, that you can make. The few dollars it costs work out to only a few cents per class. Most guides have detailed outlines or summaries of each

chapter as well as extensive sets of review questions that help you to determine how well you have mastered the material. If you cannot answer the review questions correctly after studying, you will probably not be able to answer questions on exams.

4. *Develop a regular schedule for study that allocates two hours out of class for each hour in.* Getting in the habit of regular study from the beginning of the semester will make sticking to it easier later on.

5. *Read the materials your instructor distributes in class!* You may be surprised, or even distressed, at what you find -- a strict attendance policy, perhaps, or a cumulative final exam (Oh, my God, how awful!). Many instructors will simply expect you to have read these materials and will hold you responsible for the information. Perhaps the only thing worse than knowing what is in there is not knowing!

6. *Learn your instructor's name and the proper course name and number* . These are potentially important pieces of information that can save considerable embarrassment later on. Also, learn the names of the author(s) of your textbooks since instructors generally refer to a text by the author's name on your exams and assignments. For example, recently I gave an assignment in which one question was, "Why do Smith and Jones [not their real names] suggest that emotional expression involves three factors?" One student wrote, with evident frustration, "Who the hell are Smith and Jones?" They were the authors of the text.

7. *From the outset of the semester, listen to or read all instructions carefully and follow them!* This step is one of the simplest and easiest ways to achieve student success, and its importance cannot be exaggerated. Sadly, an unfortunate number of students lose significant course credit simply because they fail to follow instructions for homework and tests. Following instructions not only virtually guarantees improved performance, but lower frustration and anxiety.

These suggestions may be summarized in a quotation by Thomas Huxley: "Perhaps the most valuable result of all education is the ability to make yourself do the thing you have to do when you have to do it, whether you like it or not; it is the first lesson that ought to be learned; and however early a [person's] training begins, it is probably the last lesson that he [or she] learns thoroughly."

Getting Started and Staying on Track: Self-motivation and Self-management

Motivation and management of our own behavior are necessary for effective action. Neither may be easy, as indicated by the all too familiar failed New Year's resolutions to lose weight or stop smoking. But many people do successfully lose weight and stop smoking by applying the same techniques that will facilitate academic success. Many students come to college already motivated to reach a specific goal, and this section will seem -- and may be -- wholly unnecessary for them. On the other hand, much research indicates that motivation, more than anything else, determines success. It is also a dimension along which many individual differences occur. Discussing motivation runs the risk of creating "self-fulfilling prophecies," things which become true merely because someone has predicted them or suggested that they might happen. Obviously the intent is not to create problems that do not now exist but to describe problems that some students have had in the past so as to help future students avoid them. After all, although we end up learning much from our own mistakes, life might be happier if we learned from others' mistakes instead of making our own!

Motivational Conflicts

Some problems occur because of motivational conflicts -- we want to do at least two different things at the same time. Since that's pretty tough to do, frequently some things win and others lose. These conflicts are "bad news" in several ways. In the first place, the things that lose are often those most important for long-term success and satisfaction. Second, academics competes with many more immediately pleasurable activities, including such things as social events and sports for which many opportunities are available. Third, college students are often away from home and external controls for the first time. Parents are not around to check on studying and assignments. For that matter, some courses will have no written assignments at all.

Course grades may be based on two or three hour exams and a final exam or only a midterm and final exam. Classes meet only two or three times a week, so that students have infrequent contact with their instructors. Class attendance, even in courses with attendance policies, is largely students' responsibility.

Students, then, have more freedom in college than they did in high school. But as humanistic/existential psychologists emphasize, with freedom goes responsibility. Increased freedom and opportunities, and perhaps limited experience in exercising personal responsibility, may lead to motivational problems. Sadly, for some the problems may become so serious that they lose their opportunity for further study by failure to meet retention standards, a fancy way of saying that they flunk out.

Intrinsic vs. Extrinsic Motivation

One difficulty in maintaining motivation for study has to do with the difference between intrinsically and extrinsically-based tasks. We engage in some activities because we find them interesting or challenging in their own right -- the motivation is intrinsic, coming from inside ourselves. On the other hand, many courses must be taken not out of interest, but to meet a requirement that comes from outside and is extrinsic. Not only is intrinsic motivation lacking, but having the course laid on us may actually evoke hostility. Knowing that a degree is contingent upon meeting a requirement may not lessen the hostility but actually increase it!

The Truth about Consequences

Maintaining motivation for study may be difficult because study and social activities have such different consequences. When you read about operant conditioning, you will see that much behavior is maintained through its consequences, and that the more immediate and tangible the consequences, the better. The classic example is a food-deprived rat in a chamber that has a lever on one wall. If and only if the rat presses the bar is a pellet of food (the

1 1

consequence) delivered. Under appropriate conditions, rats readily learn to press the bar. But if delivery of the food is delayed, then the rat may not learn to press the bar easily or at all. Now let's consider the typical academic situation. Study behavior should occur on a regular basis, but tests occur only infrequently. Thus, consequences for study -- reinforcement for high grades, punishment for low ones -- are remote. Even consequences for test-taking are remote since you may not receive your grade for some time after the exam. And grades, high or low, are hardly something tangible that you can get your hands on.

Finally, consequences for grades, such as job opportunities, are years down the line. Social activities, on the other hand, both are intrinsically interesting and have positive and immediate consequences. Saying no to an invitation in order to study may be immediately punished by derogatory remarks by friends.

The Role of the Hidden Curriculum

Given these problems, who should be surprised that developing and maintaining regular study behavior may be difficult? But here is where one of the most important aspects of the so-called "hidden curriculum" comes in. The hidden curriculum refers to things which students should learn in college but which are not part of their formal program of courses. After all, one purpose of a college education is what was referred to above -- learning to do what has to be done when it has to be done even if you would rather do something else!

Fortunately, many college courses, psychology among them, are of intrinsic interest to most students. But even if not of intrinsic interest, courses may be of crucial importance to meeting some long-term goal. You may simply want a good job that requires a college education, certainly a long-term goal for freshmen. Whether or not you find particular courses interesting, you should have great motivation to do well in order to reach that goal. The basic question is, how can we develop and maintain the motivation -- and appropriate behavior -- to reach long-term goals when short-term goals so frequently conflict? The answer may be to use some well-established principles of motivation and learning that are important to success in other activities, like sports.

Steps to Self-motivation and Self-management

1. *Write down both long-term and short-term goals.* If you have a specific career goal, write it down! If you know that you want to be able to do certain things after graduation, write them down. For this purpose, focus on those goals that depend upon successfully gaining a college education. Then write down the short-term goals needed to meet the long-term ones. Here, focus on grades needed to reach those goals: What goal have you set for each course you are taking? Be realistic! Goals set too low don't provide motivation; those set too high virtually guarantee failure. Keep your written goals where you regularly see them.

2. *Motivate yourself to reach those goals.* Write down the positive effects of reaching your goals and the negative effects of failing to reach them. Enlist social supports for added motivation; these may include family, friends, or significant others. Consider effects of success or failures on others as well as on yourself. For example, students frequently don't know that if they lose full-time student status, they may not qualify for inclusion on their parents' medical insurance. This seemingly trivial matter assumes more importance when the cost of individual health coverage is considered (easily $100 monthly).

3. *Identify and measure specific behaviors needed to reach your goals.* Study behavior will be the obvious one to reach the goal of good grades. But important questions are, how much study and what type? Keeping written records of study time helps to monitor your behavior. Remember that six hours of study weekly may be expected for each course. (Sitting in front of the textbook while daydreaming or watching TV doesn't count!) Consider the material on studying in following sections in this booklet.

4. *Arrange your environment to facilitate study.*
Find a quiet place away from distracting factors that is
associated with study and not social behaviors. One reason
for studying in a study room or the library is that
distractions, including friends inviting you to some get-
together, are minimized. Set a regular schedule for study as
you would practice for a sport. Simply establishing study as
a regular habit helps to maintain it.

Start a study group in your class. "Peer learning" is
an important current concept in education, and one which
you can certainly apply yourself. But watch out that your
study group doesn't become a social group, which is
obviously self-defeating. Effective use of study groups
requires self control and direction. One possible solution is
to set up a reward system in which members of the group
go out together after a good study session.

5. *Monitor your self messages.* What do you hear
yourself saying about school, studying, exams, etc.? What
do you hear yourself saying about yourself? What is the
first thing that you hear yourself say in the morning? One
frequently overlooked aspect of what we say both to
ourselves and to others is that someone is always listening --
ourself. And as we tend to listen to what others say, so do
we tend to listen to ourselves.

Although unrealistic positive messages may be
unhealthy, the negative ones are the most destructive. When
you hear a negative one, ask if it accurate. Many negative
self statements are so exaggerated ("There's no way that I
can pass this test!" or "I'm as dumb as a stump") that we
would be furious if someone else said them to us. One key
to better performance and greater self satisfaction in general
is to replace negative self statements with more positive
ones.

When you hear a negative self statement, try saying
to yourself, "Stop! This thought is untrue and is only going
to hurt me," and then replace it with a more positive one. As
is well known in sports, positive attitudes do lead to positive
performance.

14

6. *Accept responsibility for your behavior*. When we make an attribution, we assign a cause for something. Attribution to external factors or even to the internal one of ability may lead to several problems. If we succeed on a task, such as getting a good grade on a test, and attribute it to the internal factor of ability ("Oh, I'm just good at that") or an external factor ("Oh, it was just an easy test"), then we are unlikely either to perceive the relationship between effort, specifically studying, and the good grade or to feel proud of the accomplishment. On the other hand, if we do poorly on a task, such as failing an exam, and attribute it to lack of ability ("Oh, I just can't do that kind of thing") or an external factor ("The test was impossible"), then we are protected from feelings of failure but also prevented from perceiving that lack of directed effort may have caused the failure. Attribution of poor performance to external factors or lack of ability interferes with motivation to change behavior. And that change in behavior may be necessary for future success.

If you have studied hard and get a good grade, you should feel proud. After all, you earned it as much as does a winner in sports. Effort rewarded does marvels for self concept and achievement motivation -- but only if you attribute performance to your own effort. Don't minimize success and maximize failure. Too many people make themselves (and those around them!) miserable by focusing on things that have gone wrong more than on things that have gone right.

The other side of this, of course, requires accepting responsibility for poor performance as well, never a pleasant circumstance. But athletes who lose rarely blame the track or the swimming pool -- they practice harder so that they will do better next time. The same thing should happen with a poor grade. Since the best predictor of future performance is past performance and since instructors' testing behavior is unlikely to change, students who do poorly on a first exam in a course should practice harder for subsequent exams. Students, being human, are likely either to attribute poor performance to a variety of factors other than their own inadequate preparation or to feel that their situation is hopeless and give up. Indeed, at least one study reported that, perversely, school children who got a good grade on the first test in a course increased their study, whereas those who got poor grades decreased their study. Sadly, future failure by those who decrease study is almost guaranteed -- and needlessly. Poor performance on an initial exam or two need not predict overall failure any more than initial loss in sports guarantees a losing season. But as in sports, the poor performance is like a warning shot across your bow -- if you don't change course, you may end up sunk. (I can mix a metaphor with the best of them....)

7. *Monitor your anxiety.* Particularly as tests and other assignments approach, keep track of how anxious you are feeling -- it may help you determine if you are preparing enough. Counseling psychologists differentiate between rational and irrational anxiety. In academic settings, if you have studied thoroughly and are reasonably confident of the material, then you should feel only moderately anxious. (Since you don't know what the exact questions are and since uncertainty itself causes some anxiety, even well-prepared students should expect some anxiety.) Under those circumstances, extreme anxiety is irrational and may call for a trip to the student development center for help with test anxiety. In most cases, however, high anxiety reflects a lack of confidence in the material which in turn reflects inadequate study. In that case, the anxiety may be very rational and sending an important warning. All too often, students avoid feeling anxious over tests by putting off studying -- studying is associated with exams, exams evoke anxiety, avoiding studying avoids anxiety. Of course, the anxiety is not really avoided, just postponed! In sum, if you are anxious, perhaps you should be and should try to do something about it.

8. *Establish rewards for studying and good grades.* So normal reinforcements for studying are delayed and intangible -- do something about it! How about trying one of the techniques common to virtually all successful self-improvement plans: establish your own set of immediate rewards for studying and promise of reward for good grades on exams. Use the Premack principle (probably described in your chapter on learning), which states that high probability

behaviors can be used to reinforce low probability behaviors. It sounds more complicated than it is, essentially meaning that we can use what we really like to do to reinforce what we really don't like to do. In other words, we can use what ordinarily may be the source of motivational problems to our own advantage -- if we are willing to exert some control over our own behavior.

What do you really like to do? Play a particular sport? Watch some television show? Exercise? Listen to music? Go out? The basic idea behind applying the Premack principle is that you: 1. Identify those things that you like to do, and 2. Establish a formal contingency between studying and doing one of the things that you like to do. For example, if you like to exercise, then a contingency might be: "I will exercise for 30 minutes if and only if I have studied for two hours." or "I will watch my favorite television show if and only if I have studied two hours." Crucial is the "if and only if"; otherwise you are likely to go ahead and do it regardless of studying. If you are a member of a study group, agree to go out later "if and only if we have studied effectively for two hours."

In addition to using the Premack principle, use self-reinforcement. Telling yourself that you should feel proud for having studied can be very effective -- "It sure wasn't fun, but I studied two hours and I'm proud of it." Try also enlisting others to provide social support and reinforcement for your studying. Be sure to notice and recognize improvement both in studying and on exams.

When you get a good grade on an exam, do something special for yourself -- Buy something that you have wanted or go out for dinner. Do something special for others -- Call your parents and tell them. They'll feel good and so will you. At the very least, congratulate yourself on a job well done!

In sum:
1. You can almost undoubtedly succeed if you want to.
2. You are much more likely to succeed if you tell yourself that you can.
3. You can use initial lack of success as a means to later success.
4. Celebrate your victories!

Listening

So, what do you do while you are in class during a lecture? Yes, yes, of course, listen and take notes. But now, what do you <u>really</u> do? Let's be honest -- take a couple of minutes to make a list. As a start, you might check to see whether your notebook has the name or initials of one (or more!) "significant other" repeatedly written in it, as do many of my students' (and as did mine). Were you really listening? Compare your list with that in Figure 1, compiled from past exercises with my students. The most striking (and perhaps apocryphal) study supposedly reported that 60 percent of the time students are in class, they are thinking about sex! (As I tell my students, I know of no comparable study of what professors are thinking about in class....) But informal surveys of students' notes indicate that whatever they <u>are</u> doing in class, much of the time it is not listening.

<u>What Students Report Doing During Lecture</u>
1. Listen and try to remember material
2. Listen and take notes
3. Read lecture topic material in text
4. Read letters/newspapers/magazines, etc.
5. Write letters
6. Study for another course
7. Daydream
8. Plan activities for rest of the day
9. Talk to friends
10. Sleep
11. Doodle
12. Draw pictures
13. Write names or initials

Figure 1

Who should be surprised? Listening is difficult, particularly listening to lecture material, and is reinforced only after a long delay on an exam. You may be expected to listen to difficult lecture material for far longer than you would read comparable material without a break. You are in a double bind -- many behaviors that compete with listening are not only easier but immediately reinforced. Consider daydreaming, reading or writing letters, or chatting with friends. When tired, in a warm room, or after a large meal, we may find sleep not only easier and immediately reinforced, but almost impossible to resist. Further, unlike reading, we have little control over the speed of a speaker's delivery -- the concept of a speed <u>listening</u> course would be great if it were not so absurd.

Further complicating the problem is that the lecture content is cognitive, dealing mainly with factual information of some kind, whereas much everyday communication is connotative, suggesting meaning apart from what is explicitly being said. "Listen to what I mean, not what I say" conveys the concept of connotative information. The emotional content of these conversations is much higher, as is the role of nonverbal cues such as voice intonation and body language. Further, the content is frequently of much greater intrinsic interest. Listening in everyday conversations may be easier not only because of mutual interest and involvement, but because of greater overall arousal evoked by emotional content. Although difficult, lecture listening may be crucial to success in your course. So let's look at some ways to do the job. As you will see, many involve ways to increase attention and reduce distractions.

<u>Steps to Successful Lecture Listening</u>

1. *Be rested.* Yes, it's obvious, but just as obviously one of the main behaviors competing with listening is sleep. Recent research reveals that most Americans, including students, are sleep deprived. Students tend frequently to get relatively little sleep on week nights and then try to catch up on weekends. This pattern wreaks havoc with normal -- and adaptive -- sleep cycles.

2. *Be prepared to listen.* In many sports, the concept of "set" is basic to success, as in "On your mark, get set...." Set is also important in at least two ways for lecture listening. First, be physically ready to listen -- on time for class, desk cleared of irrelevant materials, notebook open, and pen ready. Second, be psychologically ready to listen -- *motivated* to get as much out of the class as possible (What are your self thoughts as you enter the classroom?) and *receptive* to the speaker's message. At one level, after all, the lecturer's goal is to help you succeed in the course by giving you important new information, explaining concepts, and providing clarifying examples.

3. *Sit near the front of the classroom.* You can reduce the chances of inattention by putting some control in someone else's hands. Doing anything but listening is more difficult if you are right in front of the instructor.

4. *Do not sit near friends.* I know, students sometimes take the same class to be with friends. But togetherness may be self-defeating for all. Responses that compete with listening are much more likely if you are in a group that has an already well-established social pattern. Why set yourself and your friends up for problems? Get together before or after class, but make class the business of the class.

5. *Take notes.* Active note taking virtually ensures attention to the lecture and reduces the likelihood of competing responses. This is one of the best and most adaptive ways to ensure listening. How to take notes will be presented in a separate section.

6. *Don't confuse the message with the messenger.* When Marshall McLuhan said, "The medium is the message," he wasn't talking about lectures. Not all instructors are blessed with an exciting or stimulating style of delivery. And even the best instructors have off days. A heavy dose of cognitive material itself makes the listener's job difficult. Further, some material is simply more complex and less intrinsically interesting than other. But turning the lecturer off, however immediately reinforcing, is hardly

21

constructive in the long run -- the material is still important and shows up on exams. I've seen students who have decided to "get back at the instructor" by doing something else in class, intentionally tuning him or her out. But who really suffers?

7. *Restrain emotion.* Students may well have a variety of negative emotional reactions during lecture. The lecturer's style alone may evoke frustration or anger. If the lecturer states a finding or position that is inconsistent with a student's belief, then the student may become angry or even hostile. This happens occasionally when the instructor presents findings that contradict what some students have experienced in their families or learned in a previous course. Their initial reaction is to denounce, sometimes heatedly, the instructor's position. But the instructor may well be correct -- new knowledge frequently replaces old -- or at least worth considering. Emotional reactions simply get in the way of listening and may make everyone uncomfortable. An irreplaceable element of a college education is being forced to confront the question, "How do I know what I know?"

8. *Monitor your behavior.* Learn to keep track of your own listening behavior by regularly asking yourself questions, such as Where am I? or What was just said? as a way to avoid daydreaming. One effective technique is to be ready to answer an instructor's question, even if the instructor never asks questions.

9. *Listen from beginning to end.* In opera, it's not over until the fat lady sings, in baseball (Yogi Berra?) it's not over until it's over, and in lecture, it's not over until the class ends. Beware of the tendency to close your notebook (and your ears) a few minutes early, anticipating the end of class. Those last minutes may sometimes be the most important -- your instructor may summarize important points from the lecture, give an assignment, or even announce an exam or quiz. You won't go wrong if you tune in from the beginning of class to the end. Not only in races does the finish count.

Taking Lecture Notes

Good class notes are one of your most effective keys to success. They will contain not only course content, but assignments, overviews of those assignments, and announcements of dates and types of exams. Life throughout the semester will be easier if you take thorough notes. Course credit can be lost and stress gained simply by not writing things down.

In addition, note taking itself facilitates learning and recall of lecture material. In one study, half of the students in a class were assigned to take notes during a lecture and the other half to listen carefully. After the lecture, the researcher collected all notes. In a quiz some days later, students who had taken notes performed significantly better than those who had not, although no one had notes from which to study. One of the easiest ways to improve performance is to take good notes -- virtually everyone can do it.

Suggestions for Effective Lecture Notes

1. *Use a loose-leaf notebook, filler paper, and separators for all of your notes.* Use separators to designate each course. If notes are all in one place, you do not have to worry about whether you have the right notebook for a course. A master schedule at the front can keep track of all assignments and examinations. Using a small paper punch, you can easily keep each course outline, assignments, and any other information in one place and with the course notes. If you do miss class, you can easily copy a friend's complete and accurate notes and insert them in the correct order with your own.

2. *Be an active (there's that word again) note taker.* Involvement with the lecturer's message will facilitate both understanding and good note taking. One way to look at note taking is that it is your main job in class, and as long as you are going to be in class, you might as well do as good a job as possible.

3. *Take full notes.* Listening to lecture is different from reading the text in several ways. The important one here is that you can go back and reread the text, but lecture goes by only once. If you miss it, chances are it is gone. Better to take too many notes than too few. After all, you can easily strike notes that you find you don't need, but if you don't note something the first time around, you will most likely not get another chance.

Good notes contain not only the lecturer's main points, but supporting evidence and examples. Full notes are important for several reasons. From a cognitive psychology perspective, main points alone may not be sufficient for understanding of the material, and the long-term goal should be understanding, not simple memorization. From a pragmatic standpoint, many instructors ask exam questions that not only call for simple recall, but also for application of concepts to examples. That is one way to test for understanding.

Key material to note includes that which the instructor:
1) explicitly says is important
2) writes on the chalkboard, or
3) presents on an overhead transparency or slide.

Terms and definitions, figures and tables, and names are all important. Consider taking notes during films and class discussions. Films frequently are used instead of, not in addition to, lecture presentation. Occasionally, a comment or question may lead an instructor to provide important additional information.

The general problem is, if you don't write it down, you will probably forget it. The general rule is, the more notes the better.

4. *Use a system for taking notes.* Clearly separate main points from supporting information. Haphazard notes can actually interfere with learning and understanding. Poorly organized notes consisting of disconnected phrases

not under appropriate headings virtually guarantee misunderstanding and confusion.

Many systems are available. Perhaps more important than *which* system is that you use *a* system, whichever works best. With a standard linear method, letters, numbers, and indentations indicate which material goes together. An example of notes on part of an introductory lecture is in Figure 2. Note that information is clearly clustered by concept. Another method of note taking that can be used in lecture will be described in the section on Pattern Notes.

Class 1
Introduction to Psychology
I. Def. of. Psy: Scientific study
   of beh. & processes underlying it.
   A. Scientific
      1. Based on research & theory
      2. Follows general principles of
         scientific methods of observation
         and explanation (covered in
         next topic)

   B. Behavior - observable res. of
      humans & nonhumans

   C. Processes of Dif. Types
      1. Psychological - perception, learning
         & memory motivation

      2. Physiological - neural & biochemical
         actions that underlie beh.

Figure 2

II. Goals of Psy:
   A. Describe responses & stimuli to which they occur

   B. Explain Beh --
      determine observable causes or provide theoretical explanation
   C. Predict what will happen in future -- impt. test of theory

III. Theoretical Approaches to Psy

   A. Psychodynamic - Freud
      1. Behavior affected by unconscious impulses & motives
         a. sexual & aggressive impulses
         b. dreams "forgetfulness", slips of the tongue reflect these impulses
      2. Adult Behavior affected by early (before 5 yrs.) sexual conflicts repressed in unconscious.

Figure 2 con't

27

5. *Use "telegraphese."* "Telegraphese" describes a period in language acquisition where children say the words that are minimally necessary for communication, as in a telegram. It's fast and effective. Notes rarely need to be in sentence form; even if the instructor reads a definition you can probably leave out several irrelevant words.

6. *Use abbreviations for both common and technical words and phrases*. For example, I use "w/" for "with." Then, "within" becomes "w/in" and "without" becomes "w/o." Similarly, "/n" means "not," so that "is not" becomes "is/n." Many words that come up frequently can also be abbreviated -- "Psychology" becomes "psy" or Y, "behavior" becomes "beh," "stimulus" becomes "s," and "response" becomes "r." Same with phrases -- "central nervous system" is "CNS" and the "information-processing model of memory" becomes "info-proc-mod" or a mere "IPM." Given that IBM makes computers that process information and that the information-processing model is modeled after computer systems, IPM may even be a useful mnemonic for remembering its important characteristics.

7. *Take notes in the lecturer's words*. Many books recommend taking notes in your own words, since putting information into your own words facilitates learning and memory. This is generally true -- the "levels of processing" model of memory hypothesizes that the more learners process material in terms of its meaning, the better they will remember it. On the other hand, notes in your own words may lead to at least three problems:

   a. You have to translate the lecturer's words into your own, and translation takes time. While you are deciding which words to use, the lecturer may already be on the next point.

   b. Translation may lead to error -- your words may not have the same technical meaning as did the lecturer's.

c. Consider whose words will appear in questions on exams and whose words instructors will be looking for in answers. I am not supporting the "regurgitation model of learning" in which students swallow what the instructor says word for word and then spit it back up on exams without any digestion having occurred. Far from it, as earlier material should have made clear. What I do suggest is that the major job in class may be getting information down on paper, with gaining full understanding left for later study. Getting the instructor's terms down is particularly important when lectures contain technical information.

8. *Add to your notes.* Since what is not written down will likely be quickly forgotten, review your notes after class, adding and revising to ensure completeness and accuracy.

9. *Don't copy your notes over.* In the first place you probably won't have time. In the second place, even if you do, you can make better use of your time. Copying is a passive activity which by itself will not do much to increase your understanding or memory of material. The problem is that you can copy by attending only to the surface characteristics of the words. Again, the levels of processing model emphasizes the need to process in terms of meaning. It's not as easy, but why waste your time? Only one of my students has really needed to copy his notes over -- his writing was so illegible that if he didn't, he couldn't read them!

10. *Integrate lecture material with text.* Notes that combine lecture and text material may indeed facilitate learning -- integration does require processing in terms of meaning. See the section on Pattern Notes.

Mastering   Textbook   Material

This section is designed to help you effectively read, learn, understand, and remember information in your textbook. It is also designed to deal in part with the question, "How can I get good grades?" It's hardly news that to get good grades, you have to answer questions correctly on exams, which leads to the question, "How can I best practice (study) for exams?" We all know but frequently overlook that being able to answer questions on exams requires more than simply reading text assignments. Mastery of text material requires at least three active skills -- learning, comprehending, and remembering.

Ultimately, our practice for exams should be as similar to taking exams as possible. At some point, or at several points, then, you should actually practice answering questions, since that is what you will have to do on exams themselves. Once again also the reminder that, as in athletics or music, if your goal is to do as well as possible, as opposed to simply get by, then you should practice regularly.

In either the memory or cognition chapter in your textbook, you will likely also find a discussion of "metamemory" and/or "metacognition," referring to our knowledge and awareness of our own memory and cognitive processes. Being aware of how you are now trying to learn and remember information and comparing that with some of the techniques to be presented here may be an important prelude to more effective study.

This section assumes that you have already completed the "browse" step recommended in the "Getting Started" section. If you haven't, please do so now -- the time will be well invested.

Preparing for Study

Following Buzan (1983), I suggest that each "practice" session should consist of two parts, preparation and study itself. As most athletes and musicians have a plan for their practice sessions, so you might make one for each study session. How long do you plan to study? How often and when will you take breaks? How much material do you plan to deal with? What are your goals for studying?

Although you might plan to study psychology for two hours total, you would be wise to study for about 30 minutes at a time. A basic psychological principle is that "distributed practice is more effective than massed practice." Distributed practice spreads study across a number of relatively short blocks, whereas massed practice crams it all into one large block. Two hours will be used more effectively if you divide it into four blocks of about 25 minutes each with a few minutes break after each than if you try to study continuously for two hours. Distributed practice reduces interference, in which material studied earlier becomes blurred with that studied later, or vice versa. (See the section in your textbook on proactive and retroactive interference.) It also reduces fatigue by providing rest periods and facilitates consolidation of information in our brains. The principle also calls for use of a relatively large number of short practice sessions spread across days.

Study will be better organized if you have a plan for breaking down a large assignment (an entire chapter, for example) into "chunks" that can each be managed in about 30 minutes. Each chunk should correspond to a single topic in the chapter. For example, in your chapter on learning, the topic of Pavlovian conditioning would be one good chunk. A plan guides your practice of particular blocks, telling you when you have completed one and should take a break (which can be very reinforcing itself!). Goals can also be set in terms of each block.

Finally, you might also set goals in terms of reasons why you are practicing this material. Goals provide motivation, and motivation evokes action, as we have seen.

3 1

Practice of academic material is difficult indeed if you don't know why you are practicing it. How is this information interesting to you? How does it fit in with what you already know? What did the instructor say about the importance of material in the assignment? If all else fails and you can find nothing of intrinsic interest in the material, you might simply remind yourself that like it or not, the material will be covered on an exam, and that you do have a goal of a certain grade in the course.

You may have realized that to complete the preparation phase, you already have to know something about the assigned material. In fact, some preparation is best done after the first step in practice itself. The preparation phase generally takes no more than five minutes. It is well worth the time.

Practice

The most frequently recommended study method is Robinson's SQ3R (Survey, Query, Read, Recite, Review) system developed several decades ago. As a result of some research in cognitive psychology, I have expanded it into the Robinson-Brown SQ4RO (Survey, Query, Read, Recite, Review, Reflect, Organize). The seven steps are briefly described below. You will read about some of the research that underlies this system in the chapter on memory in your textbook.

Survey

An overall survey of the entire assignment enables you to complete the preparation phase described above, including breaking the assignment down into meaningful chunks to serve as study blocks. The survey also provides "advanced organizers," terms and phrases that help guide subsequent study. Use of advanced organizers itself facilitates memory of material, as indicated by the many studies in which subjects (usually college students) remember more about a passage if it had an informative title than if it had a neutral one.

32

The survey consists of several steps:
1. Read the chapter outline, if any, or the detailed outline provided in the student guide.
2. Read the chapter summary, which contains the most important information in the chapter.
3. Survey the chapter, reading headings and subheadings and looking at figures and tables.
4. Repeat step 3, but in addition skimming the text to identify the topic sentence of each paragraph. The topic sentence contains information most related to the preceding heading or subheading. It may not be the first sentence, which frequently is a transition or introductory one. After doing the survey, complete the preparation phase, particularly determining chunks to be studied one at a time.

Except as indicated, the remaining steps deal with individual chunks.

Query

Asking questions about assigned material is useful because it both makes learning similar to test taking, in which you also answer questions, and provides motivation to understand the material, since we like to have answers to our questions. Most research indicates that the best way to study for any exam is as though it were going to be short answer or essay, so the query step is useful even for multiple-choice exams. Turn headings and subheadings into essay or short answer questions as you look over the material ("Describe four different approaches to the study of psychology."); ask identification questions about terms and names ("Who established the first experimental psychology laboratory?"); use the review questions in your study guide.

Read

Read the material with the goal of attending to advanced organizers -- headings, subheadings, comments in the margins, etc., and answering your questions. Be sure to study figures and tables and integrate them with the text. Use symbols to indicate in the margin particularly important (!) or unclear (?) passages. After reading the whole chunk, reread unclear passages to improve understanding. Work through explanatory diagrams step by step to ensure understanding of concepts. This task will be particularly important when the authors are describing the way in which certain phenomena occur. For example, you will almost certainly have to study the diagrams along with the text in order to understand Pavlovian conditioning. I urge you not to underline at this step since you may not be able to identify the most important phrases and sentences until you have read through the entire assignment.

Recite

Now the hard part -- Attempt to answer the questions you asked in the query stage with the book closed. (As will be stressed below, if you study with the book open you are really best prepared for open-book exams. How many of your exams will actually be open book?) Try to give organized and complete answers, and beware the trap of saying to yourself, "Oh, I know the answer to that one," without giving the answer. Recitation is important not only for identifying material that needs to be restudied but for helping to get the material into long-term memory in an organized way. One value of the questions is that they help provide retrieval cues that will help you recall the material later during exams. This stage can be very usefully done in pairs or small groups with people taking turns asking and answering questions.

Review

Go back over the material to reinforce learning and to study unclear passages. Be sure to deal with material that you could not remember when trying to answer your questions. After all, if you could not remember the answer, then how likely is it that you will on an exam? Only now should underlining be done, and then only sparingly. If much material is underlined, then the non-underlined material may actually be highlighted!

Reflect

Think about the material: how does it fit in with what you already know? The more you can integrate new information with old, the better. Does it complement or contradict what you already know? As in lectures, text material may occasionally conflict with what you have learned earlier, either informally or in high school courses. For a variety of reasons, your college-level material is likely to be more current and accurate. If unaware of contradictions, real or apparent, then you may give answers on exams based on what you "knew" before the course rather than on what you learned during the course.

Finally, what does the information mean to you? How can you make it of value and thus more relevant?

Organize
Learning material that is not organized or meaningful in some way is difficult and frustrating. Putting material into meaningful "chunks" will support learning and memory. Determining the hierarchical organization of concepts under headings and subheadings is an effective use of advanced organizers. Ensuring that you have material tied to its correct heading is one check. For example, Freud's theory can be described in terms of, among others, structures, dynamics, and stages. You will probably need to know that id, ego, and superego are the three structures and that the id operates on the basis of the "pleasure principle." Hierarchically, from most general to most specific, Freud's theory of personality is made up of structures, dynamics, and stages; one structure is the id; and the id operates on the "pleasure principle."

Organizing material that appears disorganized or nonmeaningful can be a challenging but creative activity. Additional tasks involve integration of text and lecture information and integration of individual chunks into a conceptual whole. Use of verbal and visual organizational aids, described in the following section, may help deal with both of these problems.

Methods for Organizing and Remembering Information

As already mentioned, meaning may be crucial for memory. The techniques presented in this section, some of which may be described in the chapters on memory or cognition in your textbook, are designed to help increase the meaning and organization of information which you may be expected to know. Described here will be some techniques useful for making meaningful and remembering both small and large amounts of information. We'll start with a couple of simple "mnemonic devices," move to more complex methods that combine verbal and visual information, and finally describe two methods to help commit material to memory.

Mnemonic Devices

Mnemonic devices, or aids to memory, have been used at least since ancient Greece. Several formal and structured systems are available, including the "method of locations" and the "peg-word" system. Although very useful, their description goes beyond the scope of this booklet. They are described in many study books, virtually all memory books, and perhaps in your textbook.

As we use hooks to grab on to things, so we can use verbal hooks to grab on to information. A verbal hook is a word or phrase that is so distinctively tied to specific information that it becomes a storage and retrieval cue. As you will see with some other techniques, humor or vividness may make the device more useful, but the crucial factor is that it be unitary -- the hook and what is to be remembered should "fit." I recommend several to remember names of important people. For example, the section on historical background may mention the British empiricist John Locke, who thought that all knowledge resulted from experience. Locke proposed that humans are born as tabula rasa, or "blank slates," on which experience stamps its effects. So, does the name Locke draw a blank? Consider Ivan Pavlov, who first demonstrated classical conditioning by presenting such things as a bell followed by food to dogs. The dogs, who initially salivated only to the food, began to salivate to the bell itself. So, does the name Pavlov ring a bell? Finally (and you may well be saying none too soon...), consider Wilhem Wundt, the founder of the first experimental psychology laboratory. So, Wundt'nt it be great to remember who was first?

Some things can be more easily remembered by making something meaningful out of their names. Let's test your memory -- What are the letters of the notes on the musical staff? Stop and think -- Remember something about "good boys"? Most of my students need little prompting to remember, "Every good boy does fine," or something comparable, for the notes EGBDF, even though they have not thought of the mnemonic for over 10 years. Successful mnemonics of this kind organize into a unit what is otherwise disorganized and confusing. Really good ones also save memory load -- the mnemonic is an abbreviation.

A couple of examples should show how such mnemonics can be developed. In studying brain-behavior relations, you may well need to know the direction in which information is carried through a neuron -- from dendrites through the cell body and down the axon. Sounds very arbitrary, something that would just have to be memorized. But if you can keep in mind that the nucleus is in the cell body, then the direction fits exactly with the abbreviation for another information system -- DNA -- Dendrite to Nucleus to Axon. How about the components and direction of firing in a simple spinal reflex arc? Sensory neuron, Interneuron, and Motor neuron form a SIMple reflex arc.

Mnemonic devices need make no sense to anyone but you -- as long as they do make sense to you, are unitary and distinctive, and are memorable. One of my general psychology students, Michael Powell, was having difficulty remembering the different models and important people associated with each one until he came up with a rather unusual mnemonic. The models (and important people or groups) were: psychodynamic (Freud), behavioral

(Watson), humanistic (Maslow and Rogers), cognitive (Gestalt), physiological (no specific person), and ethological (Lorenz). He developed a mnemonic that combined the models and the people, as shown in Figure 3, which he remembered by actually pronouncing the nonsense words with "humor" as a link between them. Each "non-o" in "PoBoHoCoPE" is the first letter of one of the models, and each "non-o" in "FoWoMoGo-L" is the first letter of the name of the person or group corresponding to the model above. Thus, the first P is psychodynamic and the F below is Freud. The "R" in "humor" is for "Rogers."

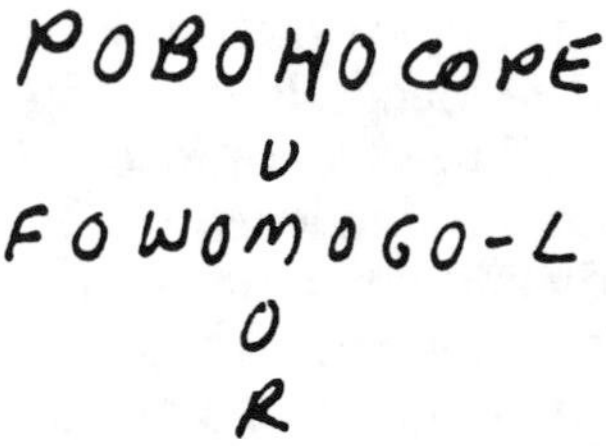

POBOHO CoPE
U
FO WOMOGO-L
O
R

Figure 3

Concept Maps

Described thoroughly by Novak and Gowin (1984), concept maps help to ensure that material is organized. A good concept map shows how concepts are related to each other, providing a "visual road map" (Novak & Gowan, 1984, p.15) of links between related concepts. Concept maps are organized hierarchically, with the most general concept at the top and more specific ones below. All concepts at a given level should be part of the more general one to which they are linked above. Although we develop the ability to form such hierarchical concepts without explicit training, the concepts are not always correct! Literally drawing a concept map helps not only to remember the information, but to check on the accuracy of our understanding of the material. At least as frustrating as not having learned something important is having learned something important incorrectly!

Many introductory psychology textbooks have a diagram of the basic structures of the nervous system that is in fact a basic concept map. Figure 4 is from an introductory psychology text.

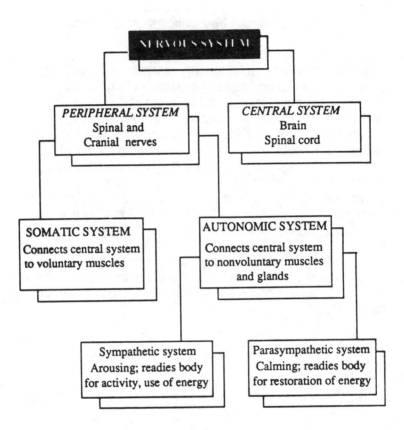

Figure 4

Note that hierarchically, the most general concept (nervous system) is at the top and that it is divided into two parts (peripheral system and central system). Knowing this map is a beginning to an understanding of the structure and function of the entire nervous system. But you can make it even more useful by expanding it, as in Figure 5, with some detail of the structures (in more or less ovals) and functions (in more or less rectangles) of different parts of the nervous system. Please note that different authors use different means of describing the nervous system. Figure 5 is a composite from several sources and for illustrative purposes only -- You should not use it to study from but as a guide to construct your own map from text and lecture information.

The concept map technique and the one to be described next have several advantages -- They enable you to integrate text and lecture material into unitary study guides and summarize the most important information on a single page, enabling you to use visualization to help to learn the material. You can also make "sub-maps" of parts of large maps to emphasize important details. Relative to the nervous system map, you might want to make a separate, more detailed one on the cerebral cortex, (part of the forebrain in Figure 5) since that is the part of the brain most responsible for complex human behaviors. You might well have the cerebrum at the top of the map and the four basic lobes (frontal, temporal, parietal, and occipital) underneath with important functions under each lobe. Concept maps may also be useful for helping to organize information on topics such as different types of learning, factors involved in motivation and emotion, and theories of personality.

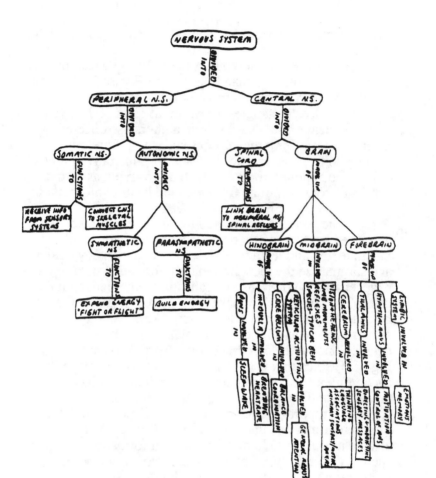

Figure 5

Patterns

Patterns, what Buzan (1983) calls "brain patterns" or "mind maps," are a quite different way of organizing information conceptually. A pattern on patterns themselves, modeled after one in Buzan, is shown in Figure 6. Although such patterns may initially appear chaotic, they are actually highly organized, but from the center out as shown in Figure 7. In Figure 6, for example, the central concept ("Patterns") is at the core of the pattern, with key sub-concepts ("Techniques," "Applications," and "Advantages") radiating out like spokes from the core. Attached to each spoke is more detailed information. Buzan has suggested that this technique better relates to our brain's nonlinear way of operating than do traditional notes. Read from the center out, patterns summarize a great deal of information on a single page. The arrows show connections between concepts that would be lost in traditional types of notes.

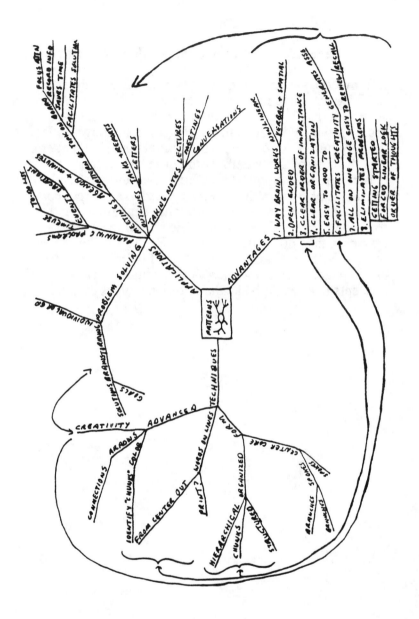

Figure 6

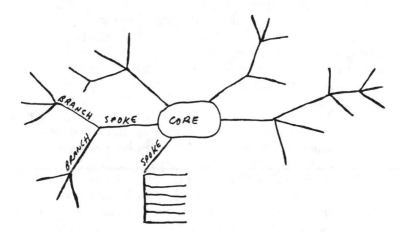

Figure 7

As a study technique, patterns may be particularly useful for dealing with material that is not hierarchically organized. For example, the first chapter in many general psychology textbooks contains information on several different concepts, typically including definitions of psychology, psychology's philosophical roots and early history, and different models or theories of psychology. The same chapter may also describe what different types of psychologists do. Initial lectures in the course may provide additional information on these topics. As shown in Figure 8, a single pattern can summarize most of the important information on these topics, integrating information from both text and lecture. The examples and information here should enable you to learn how to use the technique with some practice. Buzan (1983) is an excellent source for more information and examples.

Once the technique is learned, a pattern of an entire chapter can be constructed in surprisingly little time (less than an hour). It can also serve as a check on accuracy of understanding, since the subsidiary parts of the pattern should correspond with those of the text. A straightforward way to begin is to use the chapter title as the core concept and the main headings as spokes. Subheadings branch off from the spokes, with detailed content tied to the branches. New information from lectures can be added to the appropriate key concept, something that is difficult at best with traditional notes. If extensive definitions, figures, lists, or other such details are needed, then a two-page system, also described in Buzan (1983), can be used in which a pattern summarizes the main information and the facing page contains details. Corresponding numbers on the pattern and facing page tell you where to find the detailed material.

Both the concept map and pattern technique do take some time to learn, but once the basics are under control, they can be used to organize a great deal of information in a relatively small amount of time. They both have the advantage of being on one page, which enables rapid study of the most basic information on any given topic.

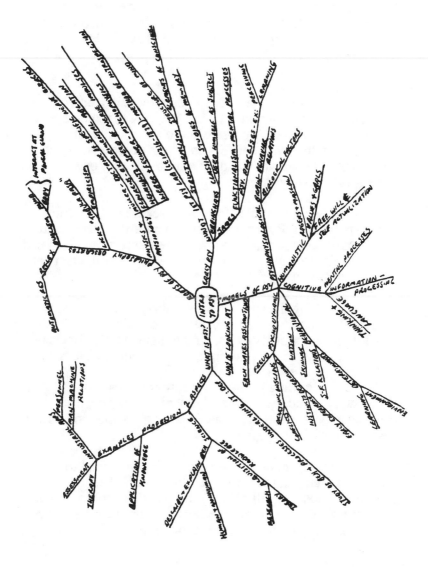

Figure 8

47

Getting the Information Into and Out of Memory

Although organization helps us to commit material to memory, some further steps may be needed to ensure that material will actually be remembered and available for retrieval when later needed.

Elaborated rehearsal
Simply repeating information over and over (rote rehearsal) is not a particularly effective way to remember material. It is also very passive and boring! Elaborated rehearsal, on the other hand, is an active process in which you recite material while adding to it in one way or another. Some of those ways are:

1. giving examples from lecture, the text, or your own experience ("Positive reinforcement involves presenting a stimulus that makes a response more likely. Oh, yes, I use positive reinforcement when I give my dog a treat when he sits down.")

2. putting the specific information into its larger context ("Psychodynamic, behavioral, cognitive, physiological, humanistic, and ethological are all models of psychology that make assumptions about human nature.")

3. integrating information across topics ("Psychodynamic, behavioral, humanistic, and cognitive theories of personality all relate to corresponding models of psychology.")

For your mnemonics to be useful, you need to remember them, and actively reciting them in their appropriate context will help ("A reflex is a simple stimulus-response relation. A simple reflex arc consists of a sensory neuron, an interneuron, and a motor neuron.")

Visualization
Some information can be more easily remembered if you simply close your eyes and try to visualize it in detail. For example, much of the material in this entire section can be related to the "information-processing model of memory"

(sometimes called the "multistore model of memory") which you may be expected to learn in the chapter on memory. The model consists of three structures and several processes. Trying to learn it by rote or even elaborated rehearsal alone may be difficult. Picturing it, however, while verbally going through it step by step may be very effective. On an exam, then, you simply close your eyes and retrieve the picture. One of the advantages of the concept map and pattern techniques is that they can be used in terms of both their verbal and visual characteristics. On an exam, if something eludes you, you may retrieve it by picturing the map or pattern.

Simply picturing complex visual material may facilitate your later recall of it. My students have found visualization to be a helpful way of remembering complex material such as important tables and figures. You may also be able to use it when trying to learn parts of the nervous system, particularly the brain.

Dealing with Exams and Assignments

This last section reviews earlier material and offers specific suggestions for dealing with exams and assignments.

<u>Overall Strategies</u>

Calendar
Problem: Assignments can be forgotten and exam dates and topics confused. Stress is gained and credit is lost. Also, since most courses have about the same number of exams at roughly equal intervals, exams tend to come in bunches, which can appear as an unpleasant surprise.

Solution: Buy a one-month-per-page calendar, punch holes in it, and put it in the front of your three-ring binder. Write all exam and due dates from course outlines on appropriate dates on the calendar. Note other assignments and exam dates as they are announced. Write down dates and times of final exams. At a glance, you can then see what is due when throughout the semester and begin to plan for what you should do when, particularly if you see in advance that exams or due dates are bunching up. Details can be noted on a sheet of paper at the beginning of the section of notes for each course or in an appointment book.

An important reminder: If you miss class, be sure to check with a classmate to see if the instructor made any announcements concerning assignments or exams.

Study schedule
Problem: The consequences of procrastination of study are obvious and all too common -- cramming, test anxiety (of the rational form!), stress, and poor grades.

Solution: Develop a written schedule for regular studying for each course -- and stick to it! One technique is to divide a piece of paper into columns (for days) and rows (for times), fill in all of your class meetings, indicating the

50

courses, and any other regular obligations such as work, and then arrange your study schedule around it. Put the schedule in your three-ring binder next to the calendar. An ideal schedule has short periods before and after each class meeting for preparation and review as well as longer sessions for actual reading and studying.

The schedule should allow at least two hours of active study time for each class hour, or six hours a week for a normal three-credit course. Yes, it really should! No, you may not need it every week (but if you regularly seem not to, then you may not be doing what you should be doing when you should be doing it!). If you cannot find six hours a week to study for each course, then you might want to consider whether your overall schedule is realistic. Wholly unintentionally, you may be setting yourself up for stress -- and distress.

A little time management
Problem: Many academic problems are (so-called) time management problems, with procrastination and failure to set priorities being particularly common. The phrase "time management" is actually, however, an oxymoron (a phrase which is a self-contradiction). As experts point out, we cannot manage time; time goes by whether we use it or not. Thus, we can actually only manage ourselves -- all time management is self management.

We may, then, choose to behave in ways which use time effectively or ineffectively. Bliss (1976) described five categories of time use:

1. *Important and urgent* tasks must be done and done now, such as exams.

2. *Important but not urgent* tasks must, or should, be done but not necessarily now. Bliss (1976, p. 18) suggests that "attention to this category is what divides effective individuals from ineffective ones." Some things in this category do not ever have to be done, and thus are not done, leading people to feel frustrated and unfulfilled. Most course-related tasks start off in this category, but all too

51

frequently do not stay there. We can easily say, for example, "Oh, I have lots of time to study for that exam; it's not for two weeks" or, "I have lots of time to write that term paper; it's not due for another two months." But, how quickly those weeks and months go by! And what had been "Important but not urgent" becomes "Important and urgent". Several "Important and urgent" tasks at the same time (bunching of exams, for example) lead to stress, anxiety, and perhaps poor performance.

3. *Urgent but not important* tasks scream "Do me now, do me now!" but do not have to be done at all and might better be left undone. Friends urging us to go out for a couple of hours is one example.

4. *Busywork* tasks are in a way worth doing but are really not important or urgent, such as cleaning off one's desk before starting to work. As Bliss points out, many are <u>diversionary</u> -- We use them to avoid dealing with more important tasks while still getting feelings of activity and accomplishment.

5. *Wasted time* activities accomplish nothing but "use time," as if most of us had time just to use! A lot of television viewing fits here. Does watching "Wheel of Fortune," or the soaps lead to long-term feeling of accomplishment or does it enable us to avoid more important activities? Television watching may be a useful relaxation. Problems arise when it becomes a dominant or dominating influence. In making up their schedule, for example, some students first fill in their favorite soaps and then arrange classes around them!

The bottom line problem is that category 3-5 activities can eat up so much time that the really important category 2 activities either move to category 1, with attendant stress and anxiety, or do not get done at all, with a variety of adverse consequences. Unfortunately, many category 2 tasks have delayed reinforcements or punishments, whereas category 3-5 tasks have more immediate, if less important, ones. Category 3-5 tasks enable us to procrastinate, putting off tasks that are ultimately very important but also in some way aversive. Procrastination is itself a complex problem, and may occur for many reasons. Generally, however, it involves some kind of reinforcement. In academic settings, the reinforcement is frequently avoidance of important but difficult and aversive tasks such as studying, taking notes, and writing papers. We just do not like to do them whether we should or not!

Solutions: Unfortunately, no easy solutions are available. Procrastination and other problems in time management may have long past histories and, like smoking and eating, may be difficult to modify. But difficult does not mean impossible, and as in losing weight or stopping smoking, the critical factor is frequently motivation. What follows are techniques that will help keep those crucial category 2 tasks under control if you have the motivation.

1. Buy a calendar and record your assignments on it, as suggested above.

2. Develop a study schedule, also as suggested above.

3. Keep a daily "To do list", essentially a set of instructions for yourself each day. Virtually all successful executives and other business people keep such a list; it is an excellent long-term habit to develop now. The list should contain specific tasks you intend to accomplish, such as "Read and study ch 1, section 1 of Gen'l Psy text" and "Do assignment on Historical Background in Gen'l Psy to hand in." List personal tasks as well, such as "Pay tuition bill." As you complete each task, check it off your list, reinforcing yourself for completing each job.

4. Use the "salami technique." Ever think about eating a whole salami at once? Talk about something that is too much to bite off! As Bliss (1976) suggests, a whole salami is actually unappetizing, but in thin slices it may be easy to swallow. So it is with many academic tasks. The salami technique breaks down large unmanageable tasks into smaller ones which can comfortably be accomplished one at a time. It helps keep category 2 tasks from moving into

category 1. "Read ch. 1," when the chapter is 50 pages long, is giving yourself a whole salami -- The task is truly unappetizing. On the other hand, "Survey ch. 1; study section 1" is a reasonable slice, and can be put on your To-do list for the day. Note that the salami technique can be used effectively only when time is available for different slices to be done on different days. If it is the night before the exam, and the different slices have to be consumed every 30 minutes, do not be surprised if some kind of gastric distress ensues!

5. Give yourself specific and meaningful reinforcement for studying, as described in the section on "Self-motivation and Self-management."

Exams: Before, During, and After

General considerations
1. What do tests test? The mistaken belief that exams test only memory leads to others -- the way to prepare for exams is to memorize, and the way to memorize is to read and reread the text and notes. Exams do measure memory, but may also tap more complex skills, such as application, organization, analysis, synthesis, and evaluation of information.

Even tests of memory may be complex since we can measure memory in several ways, recognition and recall being most important here. Recognition requires you only to match a piece of information currently present with something stored in memory. Recall requires you actually to retrieve information from memory. Rereading material prepares you only for recognition tests -- and does not prepare you well for them! Even multiple-choice questions, which ultimately require you to recognize the correct (or best) answer, may require more complex processing along the way.

For example, compare the following two multiple-choice questions dealing with difference thresholds, the detection of differences between stimuli:

(1.) Weber's Law states that:

    a. $\Delta I + I = k$
    b. $\Delta I \times I = k$
    c. $\Delta I / \Delta = k$
    d. $\Delta I / I = k$

(2.) Holding weights in her hand one at a time, Jane can reliably discriminate a 23-gm weight from a 20-gm standard. What gram weight should she be able to discriminate from a 60-gm standard?

    a. 60
    b. 63
    c. 66
    d. 69

To answer question 1, you need only recognize the correct formula. You do not even need to know what Weber's Law deals with. On the other hand, to deal with question 2, you have to analyze the statement to determine that it deals with difference thresholds, recall that Weber's Law concerns difference thresholds, recall Weber's Law itself, apply the formula to compute the answer, evaluate your answer relative to the formula, and finally recognize the choice that matches your computation. (In both cases, the correct answer is d.) Clearly, although both questions deal with the same topic, number 2 is more complex.

If study has been directed toward only recognition, then you may not be prepared for more complex questions that may be a significant part of the total exam. Further, as Pauk (1989) has noted, when going over their book and notes to check answers after an exam, students frequently discover that they had the correct answer underlined and had studied it, but missed the question on the exam! At some level, they "knew" the answer to that question but only under their conditions of study -- with the book open. Pauk suggests that they have learned to the level of recognition but not recall. This common problem is one of the main reasons

55

for the suggestions in this booklet. Unless your study behaviors include those needed in testing, you may well have trouble on exams.

2. Anxiety -- rational and irrational. A brief reminder that students who are highly anxious about a test frequently should be -- they are not well prepared and know it. The anxiety is a warning of potential problems. Unfortunately, when the anxiety is followed by a low grade, the student has even more to be anxious about. A "vicious circle" can develop in which anxiety is followed by failure which increases anxiety which makes future failure even more likely. Further contributing to the problem, when the student does try to study in the future, the setting, being associated with failure, may evoke anxiety, leading the student to avoid studying as a way to reduce the anxiety. Sadly, as we have pointed out earlier, this even more vicious circle may lead to ultimate failure. Fortunately, a cure is possible, but one which will require effort (using the suggestions in this booklet) and perhaps outside help (your Student Development Center).

3. Dangers of cramming. We have already discussed the problems associated with massed practice. Cramming is massed practice at its extreme. And it is uncomfortable at the very least. After all, cram literally means to force more of something into someplace than it normally holds. When we talk about having something crammed down our throats, we are describing an unpleasant event! (You may have even more graphic images....) Confusion and stress are almost inevitable outcomes of cramming for exams. In courses with cumulative final exams, cramming poses another risk -- even if successful for an hour exam, it does not involve the kind of active processing that leads to material being effectively stored in long-term memory. Thus, students who cram for individual exams may need to relearn much of the course material to prepare for the final exam. Given the sheer amount of information to master, cramming is even less likely to be successful.

Test taking strategies

Effective test taking involves using certain strategies before, during, and after exams. Where one has been already discussed in detail, it will only be listed here.

1. Pretest strategies: Long term.

a. Follow a regular study schedule, using spaced practice.
b. Complete assignments on schedule.
c. Take complete and organized lecture notes.
d. Review class notes and integrate them with reading regularly.
e. Use an active system for studying, such as the SQ4RO.
f. Study as though you had pop tests in all courses.

2. Pretest strategies: Review for exams.

a. Use a study group to review for the exam.
b. Make sure you know what material is covered on the exam.
c. Ask your instructor for sample questions or a practice test.
d. Attend closely to any instructor-generated review.
e. Use active review skills in studying -- Ask and answer possible questions.
f. Study as though the exam will be essay and short-answer questions. Research shows that students do better even on multiple-choice questions if they prepare for broader questions that require recall of information. If you know general concepts well, you will be more likely to be able to deal with details than if you focus on the details themselves.
g. Get a good night's sleep before the exam! Yes, I know, easier to recommend than to follow, but why do you suppose all books like this make the same recommendation? Fatigue interferes with

concentration and complex problem solving.

3. Pretest strategies: Just before exam.

a. Don't drink lots of coffee or cola drinks! (They are diuretics--and may lead you to want or even need to do something other than attend to the exam...)
b. Take a watch so that you can monitor and allocate time.
c. Be on time. If late, you may miss important instructions that are not on the exam. At the least, your anxiety will probably be raised.
d. Give yourself a positive "pep talk" on the way into the exam.
e. Be set to take the exam.

4. General test-taking strategies.

a. Read and follow all instructions and all questions carefully. Again, this is a simple but important key to success. Too often, students lose credit because they failed to see a word such as "not" in a question.
b. Answer the questions that are asked, not the ones that you wanted asked.
c. At the beginning of the exam, allocate time to each question and then check during the exam to make sure that you are on track. Having to rush through the last part of an exam under time pressure is neither fun nor effective!
d. Work as rapidly as you can, but as carefully as you can. Leave difficult questions and return to them if you have time. Both dawdling over and rushing through questions can be very risky.
e. Check over answers carefully if you have time. Look for careless errors, omitted words, and mismarked answers. You

may find that information from later
questions leads you to see an error in an
earlier answer.
f. If a question is confusing or just doesn't
look right, ask the instructor. Occasionally
instructors make errors or fail to detect
typographical errors.

5. Multiple-choice (m/c) and true-false (t/f)
question strategies.

a. On m/c questions, be sure to read the entire
statement and all choices carefully before
answering. Single words can be crucial.
You are generally to choose the best answer,
not the correct answer. Two answers may both
be correct to some extent, but one better.
b. On m/c questions, solve for the best
answer rather than try to eliminate
incorrect answers. Only if you are unable
to identify the best choice should you use a
process of elimination.
c. Don't choose answers just because they
are complex or "look good." They may be
distractors to catch the unwary.
d. Do not answer on the basis of chance -- "It
must be time for a 'false' to be correct."
e. Attend carefully to words like "all,"
"always," and "never;" they generally
indicate a false answer or incorrect choice.
An exception is the choice "All of the above,"
which may be correct.
f. Don't read additional information into
statements or choices. Treat each question
independently unless the instructions tie
them together. Questions should stand on
their own. If they seem incomplete, check
with the instructor.
g. After you have finished the exam, check
over your answers carefully, looking for
errors and mismarked answers. A
particularly controversial area of research

now concerns the question of whether or not students should change answers on multiple-choice questions. Although results are mixed, one finding that is fairly consistent is that the old recommendation not to change answers is simply wrong. Answers obviously should be changed if rereading reveals that the original interpretation of the item was incorrect. Further, if rereading suggests that your original reasoning or memory was faulty, then you should go over the question again. Similarly, you may find that information on a later question leads you to question your answer to an earlier one.

6. Post-test strategies. Because of the overall aversiveness of test-taking situations and the anxiety attached to them, students frequently avoid doing things after an exam that could help them in the long run. Exams tend to be treated as "completed tasks," never to be dealt with again. And of course once an exam is over, it is over. But you may be able to learn something from one exam that would help on future ones. Thus, these suggestions are designed to help you use experiences from one exam to help improve performance on following ones.

a. Don't kid yourself. If your first grade was lower than you would like, and you make no changes in your learning and study behaviors, chances are that subsequent grades will be similar. After all, the likelihood that your instructor will change his or her testing methods is low. Other things equal, the best predictor of future behavior is past behavior.

But initial poor performance does not have to predict future poor performance. Students who accept a poor first exam grade as a warning shot across their bow and change direction (and you thought that you had seen the last of that metaphor....) can improve dramatically. Routinely, students in my general psychology classes who get a D or even F on the first exam change their study techniques and end up with a C or B in the course.

b. Most important (and most aversive), evaluate study and test-taking performance. Saying "If only..." does nothing except lead to depression -- "If only I had studied more...", "If only I hadn't gone out so much...", or "If only I hadn't cut class before the exam...." But as Bliss (1976) points out, "If only" can usefully be replaced with "Next time" -- "Next time I will attend class and plan my study." But "next times" have to be planned and have to come to awareness in time. One suggestion: Write an "after-action report" (see Bliss, 1976), summarizing what you did well and what needs improvement and file it where you will be sure to see it well before the next exam.

If you did well, you may also want to write an after-action report to remind yourself to do the same kinds of things on subsequent exams.

c. Evaluate your study techniques relative to recommendations in this booklet. If you did not do as well as you would have liked and are not using techniques like SQ4RO, maybe it's time to give them a try.

d. Listen carefully to any in-class review when exams are handed back. Instructors will sometimes virtually announce what may come up on the next exam and may also give general suggestions for improving performance.

e. If you made an honest attempt and still did

not meet your expectations, then talk with your instructor to see if he or she can help you. Instructors generally are much more receptive to students who genuinely are looking for ways to improve as opposed to those who just complain about the exam.

Some Final Words

Thanks for reading all the way through. That's a good start, and I hope it helps. But remember that reading this booklet by itself will do you little good. What will make the difference is applying the approach and techniques we have described. You might keep the booklet handy to refer to during the course. After all, if you don't use it now, you may want to later on.

You are starting in a fascinating course, an opportunity to learn something about why we do what we do. I hope you enjoy it and learn from it. You should expect by now that I am not going to wish you good luck (you don't need it!), but I do wish that your efforts are well rewarded.

References

Bliss, E. C. (1976). <u>Getting Things Done</u>. New York: Bantam.

Buzan, T. (1983). <u>Use Both Sides of Your Brain</u> (Rev. ed.). New York: Dutton.

Pauk, W. (1989). <u>How to Study in College</u> (4th ed.). Boston: Houghton Mifflin.

ISBN 0-205-13184-0

H3184-2